Mitchell Symons was born in 1957 in London and educated at Mill Hill School and the LSE, where he studied law. Since leaving BBC TV, where he was a researcher and then a director, he has worked as a writer, broadcaster and journalist. He was a principal writer of early editions of the board game Trivial Pursuit and has devised many television formats. He has written over forty books. He won the Blue Peter Award for Best Book (with Facts) in 2010 and 2011.

Penny Symons was an award-winning journalist on the *Guardian* and the *Washington Post*. An author in her own right, she has also co-written several books with her husband, Mitchell.

Also published by Macmillan Children's Books

Philip Ardagh's Book of Howlers, Blunders
and Random Mistakery

Why Is Snot Green?
and other extremely important questions
(and answers) from the Science Museum
by Glenn Murphy

Phenomenal! The Small Book of Big Words!
by Jonathan Meres

I'M 8

I've Burped 40,908 Times!

MITCHELL SYMONS
AND PENNY SYMONS

Illustrated by Jane Eccles

MACMILLAN CHILDREN'S BOOKS

First published 2011 by Macmillan Children's Books
a division of Macmillan Publishers Limited
20 New Wharf Road, London N1 9RR
Basingstoke and Oxford
Associated companies throughout the world
www.panmacmillan.com

ISBN 978-0-330-51768-3

1 3 5 7 9 8 6 4 2

A CIP catalogue record for this book is available from
the British Library.

Printed and bound in the UK by CPI Mackays, Chatham ME5 8TD

CONTENTS

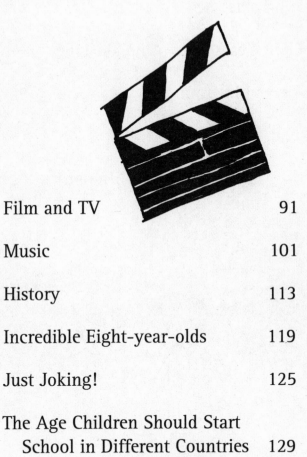

INTRODUCTION

Hello and welcome to a very special book. This is the first book for eight-year-olds that's actually *about* eight-year-olds.

You have something in common with every other boy and girl who's reading this book: you are eight years old. (If you're not, then you should stop reading right now!)

A lot of people – especially the sort of grown-ups who forget that they were once children themselves – think that being eight is just about going to school and playing at home. But sometimes eight-year-olds do extraordinary things, and you'll find out about them in this book.

As you read the stories and marvel at the trivia, remember that the people in this book were all eight when they did something memorable – just like you.

Make the most of this year: you'll never be eight again. But don't worry – there's another book in this series for nine-year-olds!

AT YOUR AGE . . .

By the time you're eight, you will, on average, have . . .

blinked 52,851,994 times . . .

taken 67,159,993 breaths . . .

brushed your
teeth 4,546 times . . .

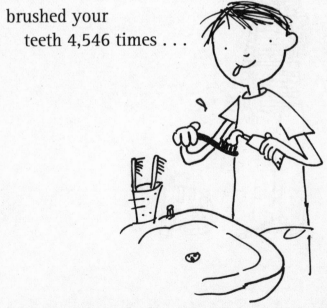

burped 40,908 times . . .

farted 40,908 times . . .

watched 4,380 hours
of television . . .

and seen 200,000 TV adverts.

You will have slept for 38,070 hours
and 53 minutes . . .

have an IQ
of 100 . . .

have laughed out loud 876,000 times . . .

and grown to
be 114 cm tall.

YOUR AGE IN DIFFERENT NUMERICAL SYSTEMS

Babylonian

Chinese

Counting rods

Cyrillic

Egyptian (hieratic)

Greek

Inuit

Mayan

Roman

FAMOUS PEOPLE

Amelia Earhart was an American aviation pioneer and the first woman to fly solo across the Atlantic Ocean. When she was eight years old, she decided to build a rollercoaster after visiting the 1904 St Louis World's Fair.

With the help of her uncle, she constructed a track that ran off the two-and-a-half-metre-high roof of the tool shed. A wooden packing box was transformed into a carriage and the track was greased with lard.

Amelia's first descent wasn't an entire success – the box broke, she bruised her lip and she tore her dress – but she was absolutely exhilarated. 'Oh, Pidge,' she said to her sister, 'it's just like flying!'

And that was the moment when the world's greatest female aviation pioneer started on her journey towards worldwide fame!

World-famous chef Jamie Oliver started cooking in his father's pub when he was eight years old.

The magician David Copperfield was already doing magic tricks at your age. He gave himself the stage name Davino.

Katie Price had already ridden her first pony by the age of eight. Within a year she would have a pony called Star on loan. She has had horses in her life ever since.

Radio presenter Simon Mayo made his first programme at the age of eight on a family tape recorder. His sister did the jingles on the xylophone!

PRODIGIES

A midwife helps mums to have their babies. But how old do you think a midwife has to be? Hope Farrelly became Britain's youngest midwife at your age when she awoke in the middle of the night to find her  mum calling her name. With no one else there, Hope helped to bring her own baby brother into the world!

At eight years of age, Xavier Gordon-Brown of Haywards Heath, West Sussex, became the youngest pupil to get an A* grade (the highest possible) at GCSE maths.

He was also studying nine other subjects including biology, chemistry and physics, playing five sports, learning three musical instruments, speaking two languages and taking opera lessons. According to Xavier's mum, he knew his times tables before the age of four and could do double-digit mental arithmetic before he started school!

Meet another clever eight-year-old: Dylan Cobb. When he was your age, he achieved GCSEs in maths and IT.

Can you imagine being a teacher instead of a pupil at your age? Well, when John Stuart Mill was eight, he was so clever that his parents appointed him schoolmaster to his younger brothers and sisters! He grew up to become a famous philosopher.

Manuel Alguacil learned to read when he was three, breezed through Tolkein's *Lord of the Rings* trilogy in two weeks when he was six and then read all the Harry Potter books. He turned his hand to writing after that, and by the age of eight he was writing his own stories. Soon he had one accepted by a publisher. It was called *Thok, the Vain Dragon,* and Manuel has gone on to write more books since then, but he wants to be an astronaut when he grows up!

By your age, twins Peter and Paula Imafidon had both passed A-level maths – an exam normally taken by eighteen-year-olds. They said that they had found lessons with children of their own age boring. Two years earlier, Peter and Paula had become some of the youngest children to pass GCSEs.

Being good at maths obviously runs in the family as their older sister Samantha took GCSEs in maths and statistics when she was only seven. At the time she was believed to be the youngest child to pass two GCSEs in one sitting.

Some consider William James Sidis the smartest man who ever lived, with an estimated IQ of 250 to 300. (You only have to have an IQ of 136 to be a mere run-of-the-mill genius, and the average person is somewhere in the 85 to 115 range.) Sidis could read at the age of eighteen months. By the time he was your age, he had written four books and was fluent in eight languages.

In 2008, an eight-year-old Brazilian boy, João Victor Portelinha de Oliveira, took – and, incredibly, *passed* – an exam to get into law school. João wanted to become a judge, and decided to take a law-school entrance exam designed for adult applicants.

The university admitted that he had passed their entrance exam and that they had enrolled him. However, they hadn't taken note of João's real age. So when he turned up on the first day of term – accompanied by his dad – he was told to go away and come back when he'd finished senior school.

'My dream is to be a federal judge, so I decided to take the test to see how I would do,' said João. 'It was easy. I studied a week before the test.'

BEECH AVENUNE

Matthew Spurgin was just eight years old when he ticked off his local council for its poor spelling. Matthew was astonished when Knowsley workmen installed road signs with a glaring spelling mistake. He noticed that new signs put up at the end of his road had 'avenue' spelled as 'avenune'.

Matthew said: 'We do lots of literature in class and I like school. I got ten out of ten in my spellings. I think Knowsley would get about nine.'

Matthew's mum said: 'He had noticed they were replacing the signs and then he said, "But, Mum, look at them – they're wrong."'

Matthew got in touch with Knowsley Council to inform them of their mistake and the council quickly replaced the signs.

In 1980, Ruth Lawrence became the youngest child to pass an O-level – an exam normally taken at the age of sixteen – when she achieved the highest grade possible in maths.

Have you ever had to stand up in front of the class and read aloud a piece of your own work? Well, child prodigy Hugh McCalmont Cairns went further than that and delivered a public lecture on chemistry at the age of eight. He was also successful as an adult – becoming Lord Chancellor of Great Britain, the person in charge of all the country's judges.

The man who created the famous Heinz company started out in business at the grand old age of eight. Yup, Henry John Heinz started his career in Pittsburgh, Pennsylvania, by selling produce from his family's garden. He made a profit and his customers came back for more.

His early success spurred him on and by the age of sixteen he had become

more adventurous. He began to dry and grate horseradish and sell it in glass bottles. He even offered to refund his customers if they were unhappy with the product.

Eventually he made more than sixty products, but he liked the number fifty-seven, so his slogan became '57 varieties'.

The huge stone lions in Trafalgar Square are among the most important symbols of London. They were created by the Victorian artist Sir Edwin Landseer, who was a child prodigy. Several of his earliest drawings, which he did when only eight years old, are in London's Victoria and Albert Museum.

E. LANDSEER

When he was older, Sir Edwin became a favourite of Queen Victoria and he gave art lessons to her and her husband, Prince Albert.

An American girl named Sahara – yup, just like the desert – has earned more than £25,000 from a book of poems that she wrote when she was your age. The book is called *If There Would Be No Light*.

32 THINGS YOU SHOULD HAVE DONE BY THE AGE OF TEN

1. Roll down a grassy bank
2. Make a mud pie
3. Prepare a modelling-dough mixture
4. Collect frogspawn
5. Make perfume from flower petals
6. Grow cress on a windowsill
7. Make a papier-mâché mask
8. Build a sandcastle
9. Climb a tree
10. Make a den in the garden
11. Paint using hands and feet
12. Organize a teddy bears' picnic
13. Have a face-painting session

14. Make snow angels

15. Bake some bread

16. Create a clay sculpture

17. Take part in a scavenger hunt

18. Camp out in the garden

19. Bake a cake

20. Feed a farm animal

21. Pick some strawberries

22. Play Pooh sticks

23. Recognize five bird species

24. Find some worms

25. Cycle through a muddy puddle

26. Make and fly a kite

27. Build a nest from grass and twigs

28. Find ten different leaves in the park

29. Grow vegetables

30. Plant a tree

31. Make breakfast in bed for Mum and Dad

32. Create a mini assault course in the garden

How many have you done already?

ROYALTY

Prince William made his first official public appearance at the age of eight during a visit to Cardiff, the capital city of Wales. On St David's Day (1 March) 1991, the young prince looked around Llandaff Cathedral and then signed the visitors' book – which showed the world that he was left-handed.

In 1993, when he was eight years old, Prince Harry dressed up in a miniature combat suit and helmet, and was photographed waving from a tank hatch during a visit to British troops in Germany. So it was no surprise that when Harry left school he chose a career in the army.

At the age of eight, the present queen – then Princess Elizabeth – told her grandmother in a letter that she had lost a front tooth. Also that she had very much enjoyed a fancy-dress party, in fact it had been 'simply lovely'. She had also learned how to ride her Shetland pony, which had been given to her by her grandfather a year earlier. At the same age,

she was a bridesmaid for the wedding of her uncle Prince George, Duke of Kent, to Princess Marina of Greece.

When Queen Elizabeth I was eight, she declared 'I will never marry' – and she didn't!

In 1185, eight-year-old Baldwin V became sole king of Jerusalem. However, his reign lasted just over a year and he died in the summer of 1186.

At the age of eight, Kangxi became emperor of China in the year 1661. He reigned until 1727. In that period, culture and the arts prospered and the population of China grew from about 100 million to about 142 million people.

James III was eight when he became King of Scotland in 1460 – after his father was killed in the siege of Roxborough Castle.

Louis XVII was declared King of France at the age of eight. He was executed two years later.

In the Bible, Josiah was eight when he took the throne of Israel. Bet that stopped his mum from sending him to bed early!

Tutankhamun was an Egyptian pharaoh (or king) who ruled between 1333 BC and 1324 BC. He was crowned at the age

of eight. Tutankhamun is famous because his tomb, in the Valley of the Kings, is one of the few to have been discovered intact. His face was covered by a golden mask. The mummy of Tutankhamun was first discovered by archaeologist Howard Carter. Legend says that a curse affected all those who discovered the tomb of this young pharaoh.

In the year 705, eight-year-old Osred became King of Northumbria, then an important kingdom in England. Osred reigned until his death at the age of just nineteen.

King Michael I of Romania was deposed as King of the Romanians when he was just eight years old. He reigned again later in his life.

William the Conqueror was eight when he became Duke of Normandy. He was crowned King of England on Christmas Day 1066. William ruled England and France until his death in 1087 at the age of nearly sixty.

At your age, you should know 26,300 words.

On average, eight-year-old girls get less pocket money than eight-year-old boys.

By the age of eight, more than a third of children own a mobile phone. Eight is also the average age for children getting their first mobile phone.

EIGHT YEARS IN AN ANIMAL'S LIFE

You are, of course, eight years old.
You could easily live until you're one
hundred. Other animals don't live as long.
Take the camel. The longest a camel lives
is fifty years, or half a human life. So
eight years in a camel's life mean twice
as much as they do to us. This means that
an eight-year-old camel is really sixteen.
Well, sort of!

Let's look at some other creatures:

If you were an elephant, you'd be eleven
   years old.

If you were a macaw, you'd be sixteen
   years old.

If you were a donkey or a crocodile,
   you'd be seventeen years old.

If you were a horse, you'd be twenty
   years old.

If you were a lion or a deer, you'd be twenty-three years old.

If you were a bull, you'd be twenty-nine years old.

If you were a pigeon, you'd be thirty-one years old.

If you were a wild pig, you'd be thirty-two years old.

If you were a tiger, cow or rattlesnake, you'd be thirty-six years old.

If you were a cat, you'd be forty years old.

If you were a wolf or a blackbird, you'd be forty-four years old.

If you were a small dog, you'd be forty-seven years old.

If you were a sheep or a goat, you'd be fifty-three years old.

If you were a fox, you'd be fifty-seven years old.

If you were a chicken, you'd be sixty-one years old.

If you were a large dog, you'd be
sixty-seven years old.

If you were a rabbit, you'd be eighty-nine
years old.

If you were a queen bee, you'd be 160
years old or dead.

If you were a mouse, you'd be 200 years old and probably dead.

If you were a worker bee, you'd be 800 years old and definitely dead.

If you were an ant, you'd be 1,600 years old and most definitely dead.

If you were a mayfly – which lives for just one day – you'd be 292,200 years old and, yes, very much dead!

On the other hand, if you were a Galapagos turtle (which lives to 200 and beyond), you'd be just four years old.

ART AND LITERATURE

Children's author Anthony Horowitz
'knew with certainty' that he wanted to
be a writer when he was eight years old.
For birthday presents, he used to ask for
books, pens and a typewriter.

The Harry Potter books are the most successful series in the history of publishing, but did you know that an eight-year-old girl was partly responsible for them being published?

The chairman of the publishing company was given a copy of the first Harry Potter manuscript by J. K. Rowling's agent. He took it home, but instead of settling down with it himself, he handed it to his eight-year-old daughter, Alice. She absolutely loved the book and told her dad that he ought to publish it. Who knows what might have happened if Alice hadn't liked it?

The famous poet Sylvia Plath published her first poem at the age of eight.

In 1880, an eight-year-old boy called Frederick Bartram Hiles fell under a tram car. Both his arms had to be amputated. But Frederick was a determined young man. He taught himself to write and draw by using a pencil in his mouth. He later went on to use a brush in the same way. His work was so good that he won a scholarship for two years' training in London and then studied in Paris. He exhibited in galleries and sold many of his pictures. Queen Victoria and Queen Alexandra both bought his paintings!

When he was eight, Walt Disney, the man behind some of our favourite films, lived on a farm. He used to sell sketches of the farm animals to neighbours for pocket money!

Before her ninth birthday, Alexandra Nichita's artwork was being compared to that of the world's most famous abstract artist, Pablo Picasso. Within a year, she'd had seven solo exhibitions, and now her paintings fetch more than £100,000 each!

The Spanish artist, Pablo Picasso, was probably the most famous artist of the twentieth century. He was also a child prodigy. One of his best-known pieces of artwork, *The Picador*, was created in the late nineteenth century when he was only eight years old.

Thomas D. L. is the eight-year-old American author of a booklet called *The Adventures of the Symbols*, in which keyboard symbols feature as characters in a story. Thomas, from North Carolina, has the extraordinary talent of being able to memorize world almanacs (books that are full of facts about the world).

Do your parents tell you off for having a messy room or an unmade bed? Well, modern artist Tracey Emin offered her own messy *Unmade Bed* as a piece of art, and it was bought by an art collector for thousands of pounds.

SPORTS AND GAMES

At the age of eight, Jasmine Hannah became one of the youngest black belts in karate, achieving the highest grade of A+ in an exam one week after her eighth birthday.

'The exam was very hard work and by the end I thought I would collapse,' says Jasmine. 'All my friends are very impressed and I really want to continue with karate.'

Formula 1 star Jenson Button, the 2009 World Motor Racing Champion, began his racing career at the age of eight when his father, a former rallycross driver, bought him a motorized kart.

Another motor-racing star, Ayrton Senna, was driving the family car (with his parents' permission!) at your age.

Dean Shiels is an attacking midfielder who has been a regular in the Northern Ireland international football team. When he was eight, he lost his right eye in an accident. However, this hasn't stopped him from reaching the very top of his profession.

Ryan Dixon was eight years old when he became a black belt in the martial art ju-jitsu. Ryan took up the sport at the age of five and raced his way through the first ten belts, completing eight in the first two years alone.

In 2009, the number-one ranked under-eight-years-old chess player in America was Tanuj Vasudeva from Newark, California. He started playing chess when he was five and now mostly plays in adult tournaments. He represented America in the Pan-American Youth Championships in 2009. (The Pan-American Youth Championships is the most prestigious chess tournament for young North and South Americans.)

At the age of eight, racing driver Eddie Irvine bought a large sack of potatoes and doubled his money selling them outside his parents' house in Newtonards, Northern Ireland. His subsequent racing career earned him some £40 million.

At your age, Manchester United tycoon Malcolm Glazer started working in his father's watch-parts business.

Alexandra Kosteniuk was a chess master when she was eight years old.

By the age of eight, Blaine Hendry, the son of snooker champion Stephen Hendry, had won sixteen trophies for snooker.

In 2005, eight-year-old Olivia Conway swam the equivalent of the English Channel in her local public swimming pool.

At the age of eight, the Ukrainian bodybuilder Richard Sandrak – also known as Little Hercules – was able to bench press 95 kg at the body weight of 32 kg.

The professional golfer Trevor Immelman scored his first hole-in-one at the age of eight.

Sam Connor was eight when he hit a hole-in-one at Alsager Golf Club on the 146-metre fourth hole. He was the youngest person to get the ball into the hole in just one shot in the club's history. However, his achievements don't stop

there. He also takes part in tournaments against much older players. The great South African golfer Ernie Els has predicted that Sam will one day win the British Open.

One golfer who has already won the British Open is Tiger Woods, perhaps the greatest golfer of all time. When he was eight, he won the Optimist International Junior World Championship. Incredibly, he wasn't playing against boys of his own age as '9–10' was the youngest age group available at the tournament. When Tiger was eight, he could go round a golf course in fewer than eighty strokes.

Andre Agassi is one of the greatest tennis players in the history of the game. When he was eight, ex-champion Jimmy Connors predicted that Andre would be a major star. Connors even said that he would retire on the day that Andre eventually beat him. Well, guess what? That day did eventually come . . . and Connors *didn't* retire!

Tennis player Venus Williams met the great John McEnroe when she was eight. They practised together and then had a short game, which he won. Venus said that she would have won if the bounces had gone her way!

Britain's number-one tennis player, Andy Murray, made his debut for the Dunblane Sports Club's (adult) third team at the age of eight.

Fred Trueman was a great cricketer and the first bowler to take 300 wickets in Test cricket. At your age, he was already playing village cricket with grown men.

The footballer Alan Smith originally preferred BMX racing to football. He won the BMX national title when he was eight.

At the age of eight, Zach Galliford, of Borth, Dyfed, became the UK's youngest first dan black belt at karate. That means he went through ALL the karate belts in an incredibly short space of time to be as good as most adults can only dream of becoming!

Former world champion boxer Barry McGuigan and his wife Sandy recently celebrated their twenty-fifth wedding anniversary. They were childhood  sweethearts and Barry first gave her a wedding ring when they were just eight years old!

When Alice Harvey was eight, she began playing squash. Nothing unusual in that, you might think. Very soon, she started winning lots of matches. Again, nothing unusual in that. So what makes Alice such an extraordinary child? She has artificial legs. Alice compensates for her disability with a unique two-handed playing style, switching the racket from left to right in the blink of an eye as she selects her shots.

Ellen MacArthur broke the record for sailing her yacht round the world by herself. When she was eight years old, she started saving her school dinner money in order to buy her first boat.

HOW TO SAY 'EIGHT' IN DIFFERENT EUROPEAN LANGUAGES

Czech: osm

Danish: otte

Dutch: acht

Estonian: kaheksa

Finnish: kahdeksan

French: huit

German: acht

Hungarian: nyolc

Icelandic: átta

Italian: otto

Latvian: astoni

Lithuanian: aštuoni

Norwegian: åtte

Polish: osiem

Portuguese: oito

Romanian: opt

Slovak: osem

Slovenian: osem

Spanish: ocho

Swedish: åtta

Turkish: sekiz

AMAZING EIGHT-YEAR-OLDS

Do you have a party piece? Perhaps you sing a song or recite a poem; perhaps you can even do a simple magic trick. Well, that's fine, but consider a Chinese man named Zhang Xingquan who can pull a car with his ears while walking on eggs without breaking them.

That's right, I said pull a car with his ears while walking on eggs without breaking them.

Sounds unbelievable, doesn't it?

Zhang, who's now a grown-up of nearly forty, started learning this stunt when he was just eight years old. What an extraordinary boy he must have been! And before you start going into the kitchen to get the eggs it goes without saying that this is DEFINITELY not something you should be trying at home!

At your age, Rebecca Shedden climbed the highest mountains in England, Wales and Scotland. She climbed the 978-metre Scafell Pike at the age of six, Snowdon (1,085 metres) at seven and then, at the age of eight, Ben Nevis (1,344 metres).

Rebecca's dad accompanies her on all climbs, roped to her because it can get really rough on the mountains at times. Rebecca says: 'All my friends are stuck in the house playing computer games, but I like the outdoors. I love the bits where you have to scramble up rocks best.' She adds, 'I want to be a mountaineer when I grow up. I would like to climb Everest one day.'

Alicia Hempleman-Adams became the youngest person to stand at the North Pole when she was reunited with her record-breaking adventurer father, David, who had just arrived there.

How tall are you? How tall are your parents? Most people's parents are less than 182 cm tall. So that makes Robert Pershing Wadlow an extraordinary person. He was the tallest person in history. At your age, he was an incredible 188 cm tall and weighed nearly 90 kg! He grew up to be over 271 cm tall and to weigh more than 220 kg.

POLITICS

In 1999, eight-year-old Joshua Browning
wrote to the prime minister asking to
become Lord Mayor of London. In
his letter, Josh said that he wanted to
become Lord Mayor so that he could take
his mum to have tea with the queen and
so that he could
cheer up the

animals in London Zoo. Do I need to tell you that he wasn't successful in his bid? Oh well, maybe one day!

Georgina Wrennall also wrote to the prime minister – and to the queen – to invite them to her eighth birthday party. They couldn't come, but at least they sent replies.

When he was eight years old, Conservative politician Michael Portillo appeared in TV commercials for the blackcurrant drink Ribena.

Britain's Labour Party was started by a Scotsman called (James) Keir Hardie. His family was so poor that Keir had to go to work at the age of eight. He became a baker's delivery boy and worked more than twelve hours a day, six days a week, for just 17½ pence a week!

FILM AND TV

At your age, actress
Jennifer Ellison was the
Junior International
Ballet Champion.

Kristen Stewart, star of the
Twilight films, began her
acting career at the age
of eight, after an agent
spotted her talent when she
performed in her school's
Christmas play.

Lisa Simpson is one of the main characters in the TV series *The Simpsons*. Although the show has been running for twenty years, Lisa has always been – and probably will always be – eight years old. Yes, even though there have been three separate episodes that focused on her eighth birthday!

When actress Jennifer Love Hewitt was eight, she joined a song-and-dance troupe named the Texas Show Team and travelled with them around the world.

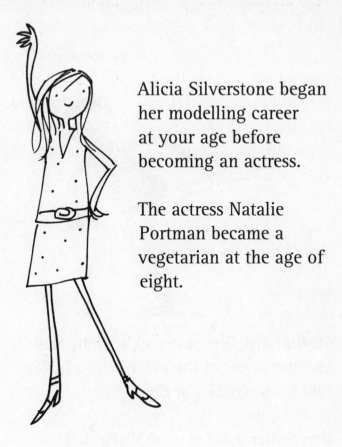

Alicia Silverstone began her modelling career at your age before becoming an actress.

The actress Natalie Portman became a vegetarian at the age of eight.

Martial arts film star Jackie Chan made his film debut at the age of eight in *Big and Little Wong Tin Bar*.

Ben Stiller – the star of *Night At The Museum* – was eight when he made his TV acting debut in *Kate McShane*.

Justin Henry was just eight when he was nominated for an Oscar for his performance in the film *Kramer vs. Kramer*. He had no acting experience whatsoever when he auditioned for the film!

Film star Ben Affleck appeared in a commercial for fast food at the age of eight. Within a year, he had also appeared in his first film, *The Dark End of the Street*.

Chances are you've been in a school play. Perhaps you were a bit disappointed not to be given the leading role? Don't worry! At your age, the Australian actress Nicole Kidman made her theatrical debut as a sheep in a nativity play. As for her costume, it was a woolly car-seat cover!

Doctor Who actress Billie Piper enrolled in the Sixth Sense theatre company at the age of eight. She started her career by appearing in TV commercials.

When she was eight, film star Scarlett Johansson made her professional debut in a play alongside Ethan Hawke. She also made her TV debut in a comedy sketch on the programme *Late Night with Conan O'Brien*. The presenter, Conan O'Brien, wasn't aware of this until Scarlett told him when she appeared on his show as a guest twelve years later.

TV presenter Anthea Turner first became famous as a *Blue Peter* presenter, so it's fitting that she won a *Blue Peter* badge at the age of eight for sending in a collection of seashells.

Malandra Burrows is best known for appearing in *Emmerdale* and as a contestant in *I'm A Celebrity . . . Get Me Out of Here*, but she's been singing and dancing ever since she was a toddler. At the age of eight, she appeared on the TV talent show *New Faces* – and won! In fact, Malandra was the youngest-ever winner of that programme.

American film and TV star Sarah Jessica
Parker won the lead in a TV production
of *The Little Match Girl* when she was
eight.

The actress Christina Ricci started doing
voiceovers for TV commercials at the age
of eight.

Film star Keira Knightley was eight when
she made her acting debut
alongside Minnie
Driver and Rupert
Graves in BBC TV's
Royal Celebration.

MUSIC

At your age,
Julia Hwang
scored ninety
per cent in
her grade-
seven violin exam. Within a year, she
was preparing for the grade-eight exam.
The usual age for entrants is seventeen,
and Julia is thought to be the youngest
violinist ever to take the thirty-minute
exam.

At the age of eight, Evelyn Glennie became profoundly deaf – she couldn't hear anything except for extremely loud bangs. Incredibly, she has grown up to become the world's most famous percussionist – someone who plays drums and all things noisy!

Pianist Jools Holland started playing the piano at the age of eight, when his uncle taught him 'St Louis Blues'. The young Holland would pound out the same tune for hours at a time in his grandmother's front room, a few streets away from his parents.

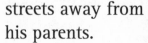

Wolfgang
Amadeus
Mozart, one
of the greatest
classical composers
of all time, composed his first symphony
at the age of eight.

Andy Williams is a very well-known American singer. He began his career singing in a local church choir, and turned professional with his three brothers at the age of eight. They performed across the United States before moving to Los Angeles where Andy – a boy, remember! – dubbed the actress Lauren Bacall's singing voice in the film *To Have and Have Not*.

Composer Johann Strauss had already composed his first waltz by your age.

Frederic Chopin, a famous composer, made his debut as a concert pianist at your age.

The modern classical composer Karlheinz Stockhausen started giving piano recitals at the age of eight. He also exhibited an amazing talent: he only needed to hear a piece once in order to be able to play it.

MUSIC

When he was eight, the singer Gareth Gates discovered that he didn't stutter when he was singing.

The singer Shakira wrote her first songs at the age of eight. Five years later, at the age of just thirteen, she signed up for a three-album deal with Sony.

Sir Mick Jagger and Keith Richards are two members of the rock group The Rolling Stones. They were both eight when they met for the first time.

At the age of eight, the American actor and country singer Burl Ives had learned the banjo and made his first public appearance at a local old soldiers' reunion. The audience liked him so much that his pre-arranged fee of fifty cents was doubled to a dollar!

The violinist Yehudi Menuhin was probably the most famous classical musician of the twentieth century. At the age of eight, he gave his first full-length solo recital and was immediately acclaimed as a genius.

The musical prodigy Yuko Ohigashi composed her first song at the age of eight.

In 1995, the eight-year-old violinist Nicola Benedetti became the youngest person to lead an orchestra in Scotland.

At the age of eight, Yuanfan Yang became the youngest person to pass the grade-eight piano exam run by the Associated Board of the Royal Schools of Music. Most students are in their late teens before they reach that level.

Vanessa-Mae is one of the world's leading violinists. Having played the violin for three years, at the age of eight she went to China to study. She says, 'I was a tough cookie and decided at eight that I wanted to be a violinist.'

Martin Kemp's acting career began at the age of eight when his mother sent him to the Anna Scher drama school in Islington, North London. But he first became famous as a pop star – in the 1980s he and his brother Gary were in the pop group Spandau Ballet, which re-formed in 2009.

At your age, the singer-songwriter Duffy kept a notebook in which she would write song lyrics and ideas for songs.

Robbie Williams made his
first public performance
in a production of *Oliver!*
at the age of eight. He
played the Artful Dodger.

The singer-songwriter Katie Melua moved
from wartorn Georgia in Russia to Belfast
when she was eight.

Britney Spears first appeared on TV – on
the *Mickey Mouse Club* – at the age of
eight.

Rhys Nichols was just eight years old when he spotted a set of dinosaur footprints that dated back an incredible 160 million years.

Rhys was strolling along the beach with his dad when he spotted the perfectly preserved 23-cm prints on a rock. The clever schoolboy immediately realized they could be from a dinosaur, and experts believe they are the mark of

a plant-eating iguanodon creature that roamed there during the Jurassic era.

Rhys's dad thought that the amazing prints were probably revealed after rocks recently fell from the cliff face. 'We are always coming down here beachcombing and looking for fossils,' he said. 'There are some other prints on the beach, but they have become eroded now.'

Sir Josiah Mason was born on 23 February 1795. At the age of eight, he started selling cakes in the streets, and afterwards fruit and vegetables, which he carried from door to door on a donkey. He grew up to be a pen-nib manufacturer and philanthropist (someone who gives a lot of their money away to help people less fortunate than themselves).

Matthew Michell, an eighteenth-century naval officer, was just eight years old when he first went to sea as a sailor.

In the eighteenth century, boys of your age joined the Royal Navy and actually went to sea!

In Scotland in 1945, working-class children at the age of eight were five centimetres taller than eight-year-olds had been in 1939. Why? Because during World War II, there was an equal distribution of food. Also, children were given free milk and vitamins to help them grow properly.

In the seventeenth century, when a person reached the age of eight, they were considered old enough to work alongside adults. For example, in the coal mines, eight-year-old boys were sent underground to work for several hours a day.

The boys were expected to work on their own – perhaps opening and closing ventilation doors for older boys who were transferring tubs of coal back and forth from the coalface. They worked by candlelight with rats scurrying around them. There were no holidays and the boys worked six days a week, every week of the year. We're all a lot luckier now!

In 1861, an eight-year-old boy called Avery Brown succeeded in volunteering for the Union Army in the American Civil War. An old soldier named Samuel Mott had encouraged the youngster to play his snare drum at the recruitment station. Like many enthusiastic young patriots of his day, he lied about his age, claiming to be twelve on his enlistment papers.

Guru Har Krishen died in 1664 at the age of eight – having been the Sikh Guru since the age of five. As he instructed his followers to build schools for religious education, most of the modern Sikh schools are named after him.

INCREDIBLE EIGHT-YEAR-OLDS

Tomas Jackson, an eight-year-old gardener from Chester-le-Street in County Durham, won first prize and the title of 'Young Gardener of the Year' in a 2009 gardening competition after creating a vegetable plot at his grandma's house. Tomas has always enjoyed pottering around the garden and growing his own vegetables – even though he doesn't like eating them!

119

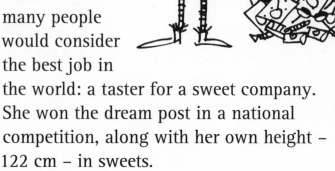

When she was eight years old, Lauren Wakeling landed what many people would consider the best job in the world: a taster for a sweet company. She won the dream post in a national competition, along with her own height – 122 cm – in sweets.

Nowadays, John Caulcutt is the chief executive of a large company, but when he was just eight he was running a shopping service for sailors in Yarmouth Harbour on the Isle of Wight.

At the age of eight, Abigail Wright's dream was to be a bridesmaid at a wedding. Her mum advertised in a local paper asking if anyone who was planning a wedding would let her be a bridesmaid. A little while later, a total stranger got in touch and asked her to be a bridesmaid. Abigail's dream came true – all thanks to her mum!

Successful American businessman Victor Kiam started making money when he was eight by selling soft drinks to people as they travelled home from work.

JUST JOKING!

'And what will you do when you grow up to be as big as me?' asked Ben's dad.

Eight-year-old Ben looked at his dad.

'Diet,' he replied.

A man walked into a pet shop and said, 'I'd like a puppy for my eight-year-old son.'

'Sorry, sir,' said the shop owner, 'we don't do part exchange.'

One day at school, eight-year-old Jack was talking to his classmate Sophie.

'Hey, Sophie, have you heard the joke about the dustbin lorry?'

'No, I haven't,' replied Sophie.

'Don't worry,' said Jack, 'it's a load of rubbish.'

THE AGE CHILDREN SHOULD START SCHOOL IN DIFFERENT COUNTRIES

Age	Country
Four	Northern Ireland
Five	England, Malta, Netherlands, Scotland, Wales
Six	Austria, Belgium, Czech Republic, Denmark (seven until 2008), France, Germany, Iceland, Republic of Ireland, Italy, Liechtenstein, Norway, Portugal, Romania, Slovakia, Slovenia, Spain, Turkey
Seven	Bulgaria, Estonia, Finland, Lithuania, Poland (but kindergarten is compulsory from the age of six), Sweden

PHiLiP Ardagh's book OF HOWLERS BLUNDERS and RANDOM MiSTAKERY

Find out how the Pope got confused with a
potato, about the footballer who ate the
ref's notebook and why it's a terrible idea
to get your name and date of birth tattooed
on your neck in this splendid romp through
the most impressive mistakes, blunders,
misunderstandings, faux pas, howlers and
universal truths that are not true at all!

Why is SNOT green?

The First Science Museum Question and Answer Book

Glenn Murphy

Why is snot green? Do rabbits fart? What is space made of? Where does all the water go at low tide? Can animals talk? What are scabs for? Will computers ever be cleverer than people?

Discover the answers to these and an awful lot of other brilliant questions frequently asked at the Science Museum in this wonderfully funny and informative book.

PHENOMENAL!

The SMALL book OF BIG WORDS!

Jonathan Meres

Discover loads of big words and what they mean!

Discombobulate asinine adversaries with your verbal guile!

Fool grown-ups into thinking you're dead clever!

Work out what the heck that last sentence meant!

Become fabulously popular and successful or your money back!*

*Terms and conditions apply

A selected list of titles available from Macmillan Children's Books

The prices shown below are correct at the time of going to press. However, Macmillan Publishers reserves the right to show new retail prices on covers, which may differ from those previously advertised.

Philip Ardagh

Philip Ardagh's Book of Howlers, Blunders and Random Mistakery	978-0-330-50807-0	£5.99

Glenn Murphy

Why Is Snot Green?	978-0-330-44852-9	£5.99

Jonathan Meres

Phenomenal! The Small Book of Big Words!	978-0-230-75193-4	£5.99

All Pan Macmillan titles can be ordered from our website, www.panmacmillan.com, or from your local bookshop and are also available by post from:

Bookpost, PO Box 29, Douglas, Isle of Man IM99 1BQ

Credit cards accepted. For details:
Telephone: 01624 677237
Fax: 01624 670923
Email: bookshop@enterprise.net
www.bookpost.co.uk

Free postage and packing in the United Kingdom